D1535230

Under the Mountain

Matt Sims

High Noon Books
Novato, California

Editor: Deb Akers
Cover Design: Bonni Gatter

Cover Photographs: courtesy NORAD and
Department of Defense
Interior Illustrations courtesy of NORAD (4, 9),
United States Air Force (15, 23, 27), Department of
Defense (20)

High Noon Books
a division of Academic Therapy Publications
20 Commercial Blvd.
Novato, CA 94949-6191

International Standard Book Number: 978-1-57128-482-2

18 17 16 15 14 13 12 11 10 09
10 09 08 07 06 05 04 03 02 01

Contents

The United States of America

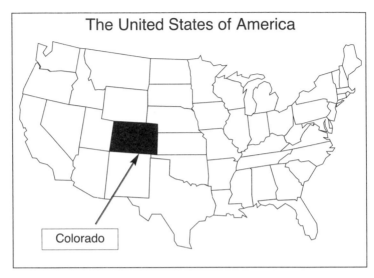

Colorado

Colorado State

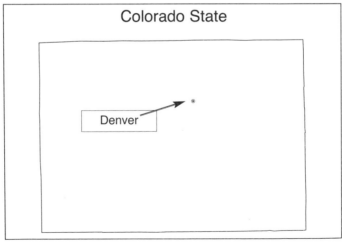

Denver

Norad

The mountain peak
turns red as the sun
sets. The place looks
peaceful. A hawk circles
in the sky.

A long black car heads
up the mountain. It
drives along a narrow

road. Is someone going for a hike? Or maybe they have planned a camping trip.

The car slows down at the end of the road. It has come to a tunnel. There is a checkpoint by the side of the road. An arm comes out of the window. A hand slips a card into a slot. The car drives into the tunnel.

Where does that
tunnel go? It leads to a
secret base called Norad.
The base is built deep
inside the mountain. A
base built inside a
mountain? That is a fact.

The Norad base was
built in the 1960s. Its job
was to keep track of all
air flights over the U.S.

The base is built deep inside the mountain.

The staff at Norad watched for missiles that might be aimed at the U.S. They could send out warnings. They could help the country get ready for an attack.

No one can go inside the mountain without a pass. Norad has always been a top-secret place.

Why build a base

inside a mountain? And how did they do it? These are all good questions. The answers might surprise you.

Blasting In

The workers set the first charge. Then they sat back. They watched the rocks explode. Boom! Rocks and pebbles flew up. The sky filled with clouds of dust.

The workers blasted

into the mountain. They did it bit by bit. They were going to make a space deep inside. It would sit under 2,000 feet of rock.

The space would be about 100 feet tall. There would be room for office buildings. There would be tunnels that ran from place to place.

They watched the rocks explode. Boom!

Miles of wire were set under the mountain. These would give the base power. Phone lines were put in. Big cables would link Norad to the world. Now they could send out warnings if they saw danger.

People would be living and working inside the mountain. Air vents had

to be built. They also
had to find ways to get
water pipes into the
base. They made sure
that Norad was safe for
the people inside.

A Cold War

Norad cost a lot of money. It was very hard to build. Why did they spend all that time and money?

Norad was built during a strange time. The U.S. was afraid it

would be attacked.
People thought the
attack could happen at
any time.

Russia (RUH-shuh)
had atom bombs. It could
drop them on our country
from planes. We had
atom bombs, too. We
could drop them on
Russia from our planes.
Each one of these bombs

would kill people for miles around.

The U.S. thought it could stay safe from the big bombs. Norad would give people a warning. Then they could hide in their basements. They would wait until it was safe to come out again.

Later, people learned that the bombs were

*Each one of these bombs would kill people for
miles around.*

much worse than they had thought. These bombs would end human life for a long, long time. No one could hide from them.

Norad did a lot to help the U.S. The base under the mountain was a very safe place. But it could not keep the whole country safe. The U.S.

also worked with other countries. This was a good way to make the U.S. safe. This is still true today.

Life Inside

Not many people know
what the Norad base
looks like. There are
very few pictures of the
inside of the base.

We do know that
people live and work
inside the mountain. We

can make some guesses about life inside the Norad base. There are rooms for people to sleep in. There are places to eat. There may be a few shops in the base. There are even places for the staff to relax after work.

We know that people walk through tunnels from place to place.

There are even places for the staff to relax after work.

There are even little trains that people can ride. It would be fun to tour the Norad base. If only we could!

Secrets of Norad

We have pictures of the "war room" in the Norad base. That is a room full of big screens. The screens show all airplanes flying over the U.S.

The Norad staff sits

The screens show all airplanes flying over the U.S.

and watches the screens.

They look for planes that do not belong there. People will check out any strange planes.

No one can get in or out of this room without a pass. The work done in this room is top secret. Very few people in the U.S. know what goes on in the "war room".

Stand Down

The Norad base has huge doors. They are three feet thick. They were made to keep out a big bomb blast.

In the 1980s, Russia and the U.S. signed a deal. Big bombs were

The Norad base has huge doors. They are three feet thick.

less of a danger. There was now less need for Norad.

In 2006, the Norad base was told to "stand down". This means that it was partly closed. There are still some jobs at Norad. But many people have moved out of the mountain.

High Frequency Words

a	get	or
all	go(ing)	out
an	has	over
as	have	that
at	help	the
be	in	there
black	into	they
by	is	to
come	it	up
does	look(s)	was
down	no	where
for	of	yes